T0207691

SCRIPTURAL TRAIL FROM EDEN

HOWARD BASTIAN

authorHOUSE®

AuthorHouse™
1663 Liberty Drive
Bloomington, IN 47403
www.authorhouse.com
Phone: 1 (800) 839-8640

Published by AuthorHouse 11/11/2019

Scripture quotations marked KJV are from the Holy Bible, King James Version
(Authorized Version). First published in 1611. Quoted from the KJV Classic
Reference Bible, Copyright © 1983 by The Zondervan Corporation.

ISBN: 978-1-7283-3508-7 (sc)
ISBN: 978-1-7283-3507-0 (e)

Library of Congress Control Number: 2019918056

Print information available on the last page.

Any people depicted in stock imagery provided by Getty Images are models,
and such images are being used for illustrative purposes only.
Certain stock imagery © Getty Images.

This book is printed on acid-free paper.

I dedicate *The Scriptural Trail from Eden* to people who are sincerely and persistently searching with a burning desire to find a satisfying truth and peace about the Triune God—the Father, the Son, and the Holy Spirit.

CONTENTS

ᴵNTRODUCTION

The Scriptural Trail from Eden summarizes and traces the evolution of Christianity from its beginning to the second coming of Jesus Christ with scriptural support to keep the reader anchored in the Holy Bible. Christians and non-Christians alike should find this book very interesting.

It is alarming to realize that the billions of people on the planet Earth came from a man and woman created by God in the Garden of Eden, and that their disobedience, which took place in the garden, is the primary reason why Jesus Christ came to bring man's salvation.

To understand the history of the redemption story and to accept Jesus Christ as Lord, Savior, and King, we must backtrack to the beginning. It all started in the book of Genesis and concluded in Revelation.

As I mentioned, *The Scriptural Trail from Eden* allows the reader to visualize the path for the coming of Jesus Christ. It places emphasis on the journey of God's chosen people and highlights how God intimately interacted and traveled with His people on their historical path for the sake of His only Son.

This book offers renewal for dedicated Christians, a better understanding for new converts, and a sense of purpose for those who may still be searching.

Points that are considered significant are highlighted and discussed, such as prophecies about the coming of Jesus Christ and the relationship between God and humankind.

We all have our own experiences when considering

Christianity. I share a part of my exciting Christian journey that strengthens my faith with hope that it may assist others in their own search to establish a relationship with Jesus Christ.

PERSONAL PATH

THE BIBLE IS A FASCINATING BOOK THAT I READ because it describes every aspect of human life. Somehow it captures our weaknesses, strengths, desires, failures, and high and low points of our lives. The Bible's teachings apply to every generation, despite how the ways of life may change. The principles embedded in this book can also become a part of our daily lives.

After two thousand years, the teachings of a man who appeared to be ordinary—yet was both God and man—left an indelible mark on humanity. Today, many people still strive to follow the teachings of Jesus Christ. The Bible is accessible to millions and can be used to self-evaluate our behaviors. Many of us look at it every day, and some will dust it off now and then or even pack it away.

We often view the high cost of an item to determine its value. The price for a Bible is low, and in many instances, it is given freely. But because it is not commercialized and repackaged like some items, it can be looked upon as insignificant. This ancient book is proven to be valuable because its teachings are passed down though many generations, which reflects how our parents, our family members, and others have lived what we consider "good lives." We realize that some of them have had a tremendous faith in God that became the primary reason for their survival. However, sometimes we tend to abandon this tradition, especially in our youth. But fortunately, as we age, we see wisdom.

The good news is that, wherever you are on your life's journey, whether you have been beaten down or you are on the top of your game and the spotlight is presently on you, the teachings of Jesus Christ can relate to your situation and improve it.

I

I grew up around family members and others who lived with a certain degree of Christianity. I regularly remember my grandmother—who died when I was a child—because of how she lived a Christian life. It seems as if she set the Christian bar higher than I can achieve. There are many people like her who appear to strengthen our communities with their consistent Christian living.

As a child, I had the privilege of experiencing different religious denominations, thanks to my mother and my grandmother. I remember sometimes standing outside a church, looking through the window with great excitement as the members praised God. I observed the functions of these denominations but did not fully understand what made them different from the others. Of course, most of them had their particular concepts of the doctrine of Jesus Christ and His teachings. However, later in my life, I studied some of these denominations to determine which one is the most comfortable for me to practice my own Christian beliefs.

II

In my late twenties, it became almost unbearable to understand how a person can be inhumane to another. As an example, I refer to the civil rights movement and the outright evil that one person may afflict upon someone else. In some cases, natural disasters or other events that have horrific effects on people and communities appear to be the responsibility of God. Many times, we question God about His reasons for not alleviating human suffering.

I seriously and dramatically questioned God to determine whether He was still alive. Afterward, I realized that He is all-powerful and merciful, and he could have ended my life due to how I approached Him in my desperation. Instead, I walked away almost tearful after recognizing that I had called out a God who is wise, understanding, and who has unconditional love for me. I also understood the war that the devil is raging for my soul.

III

I have a limited understanding of some non-Christians' views about God. I accept that they also are children of God on their own spiritual journeys. I feel that they are sensitive and remarkable people who sincerely question the existence of God. God is big enough to protect Himself and deal with any challenges from His creation. After all, I am not a perfect being and am in no position to judge anyone.

The early stages of my adult life helped me to better understand what could drive people to develop non-Christian viewpoints. The awful life experiences that we sometimes have are heartbreaking and unthinkable. Some of us are still going through a healing process that may affect our views about God.

I can relate to the apostle Thomas, who walked with, talked with, and ate with Jesus. Then he witnessed the unimaginable: the suffering and death of his idol and leader—someone he looked upon as king. When Thomas returned to the other disciples and found out that the crucified Jesus had visited them, he did not believe them. Because, he could not accept that his Lord was alive since he wasn't present when Jesus visited the disciples the first time.

John 20:27–28 explains what transpired between Thomas and Jesus the second time Jesus visited the disciples. They remained in a closed room because they were afraid of the Jews. Jesus stood in front of Thomas to fulfill Thomas's request that he had made eight days prior: for Him to satisfy his doubts that Jesus was alive. Jesus invited Thomas to place his finger in His hands and to put his hand into His side. After Thomas had done what Jesus asked, he said, "My Lord and my God" to Jesus.

In my opinion, Thomas's request was human, and it did not make him lesser than the others. I, too, was like him in many ways. I sincerely presented my doubts to God about his existence, and He responded gently and informatively. There are a lot of us like Thomas, waiting for an assurance that Jesus Christ is a living God. If you do not harden your heart, God may also come to you.

IV

I grew up accepting that the Bible is the Word of God. Therefore, when I had my doubts about God, my first instinct was to read the Bible to determine if it was genuine. My position was quite simple: if I proved that the Bible was an authentic book, then I ought to accept it as the Word of God.

As I read the Bible for the first time, I noted a lot of questions I had about what may be considered inconsistencies and contradictions. During my second reading, I found answers to most of my queries. Sometimes this happened because of my interpretation, the author's tradition, unintended prejudices, or the writer's viewpoint.

During my third reading, I referred to religious documents and engaged others in their viewpoints to assist me in my understanding. At the end of the third reading, I knew that the Bible was the Word of God.

I eventually became convinced that the entire Bible is consistent with its teachings of redemption and is related to me in so many ways. For the first time in my life, with all my anti-Christian actions, I formed a personal relationship with God. I am convinced that the Holy Spirit inspired the writing of the Bible and that God is as alive today as He was yesterday. As my spiritual journey developed, I started to pray consistently and had informal talks with God during the day. Somehow, it seemed as if my communication with God was one way. I did not feel as if He acknowledged my prayers or responded to them. I soon developed a feeling of emptiness and frustration because I wanted two-way communication and to have a sense of intimacy with Him.

I tried many direct approaches to form this relationship with Him, but I thought that I was not connecting. In my desperation, I realized that God lives in an active spiritual world and that there is a protocol system that may be beyond our imagination.

I reflected on the patriarchs from heaven who were talking with Jesus on Mount Tabor and were witnessed by the apostle Peter and others, as recorded in Luke 9:30–31: "And, behold, there talked with him two men, which were Moses and Elias: Who appeared in glory, and spake of his decease which he should accomplish at Jerusalem."

This event helped to convince me that there is an active spiritual world. These men did not randomly appear from the spiritual world; Moses represented the period of the Law and Elias the prophets.

I also reflected on when Moses requested to see the face of the Lord, and the Lord made accommodation for Moses to see Him, as written about in Exodus 33:18–23.

After these reflections, there was no reason for me to disbelieve that an active spiritual world existed. Then, in the presence of God, I requested that my favorite saint assist me in feeling the connection with Jesus.

After a short time, I developed what I consider a two-way relationship with God in my spirit, and I felt confident that even my whisper was acknowledged. In my newly formed intimacy with Jesus, I experienced some spiritual encounters on my Christian journey that are difficult for others to understand.

Every day, I notice the beauty of God's creations and marvel at their performance. I am humbled to be a part of God's universe that has me in constant awe. As I think about His creation, which I know is both spiritual and physical, I sometimes focus on the spiritual world where God resides.

I acknowledge the existence of an eternal God that consists of the Father, the Son, and the Holy Spirit, and how each has unique functions. The extent of these functions is not understandable by human imagination. However, I think that God may unveil some of the mysteries to whomever He wishes, as He did with Moses.

My research also led me to find out about the many biblical writers who wrote their stories over sixteen hundred years—stories that remain with us today. They were like me. I was not familiar with the Holy Spirit at the time when I became aware of the systematic layout of and the themes used throughout the Bible. Once I read it, however, I was convinced that it could have been only the Holy Spirit who inspired these writers over such a period.

I could not come up with any other explanation but the intervention of the Holy Spirit after finding out that these writers came from every social status, including statesmen and peasants, kings, herdsmen, fishermen, priest, tax-gatherers, and tentmakers. Most of the writers were unknown to each other. They were educated, uneducated, Jews, and Gentiles.

Exodus 4:15 reminds us of how God can speak to anyone He wishes, similar to how he reaassured Moses with his fears of approaching Pharoah. God promised that He would put words in the mouths of Aaron and Moses as they spoke with Pharoah.

V

The first book of the Bible began with God creating the garden for humans' comfort. Then, the devil entered it and persuaded Eve to be disobedient to Him. After this defiant act, God issued His punishment and began the process of redeeming humankind through His Son, Jesus Christ, to reform our broken relationship with Him.

The Bible is a book about the redemption of man. During the redemption process, God traveled with Abraham's descendants, whom He ordained to bring His Son into the world to redeem humanity from sin and death.

In *The Scriptural Trail from Eden*, it is my pleasure to highlight this story with relevant scriptures that I feel will provide support for my biblical points and the authenticity of the Holy Bible.

I invite you to pull out your bible and to journey with me as I take you through this book, which states some of my biblical views that may have some effect on your Christian outlook.

On our journey, we ought to accept that our imperfections give us a choice either to reject or to accept the path that God's only Son has prepared for our salvation.

Based upon our free will, our decisions may be good or evil, and the right choices sometimes relate to the teachings of Jesus Christ that have been with us from the beginning, as recorded in John 1:1: "In the beginning was the Word, and the Word was with God, and the Word was God."

Our evil decisions are sometimes related to the devil, who has also been with us from the beginning, as recorded in 1 John 3:8: "He that committed sin is of the devil; for the devil sinneth from the beginning. For this purpose the Son of God was manifested, that he might destroy the works of the devil."

ꝏFALLEN

ꝏAs I reflect on the history of the salvation story, I found myself in the Garden of Eden, where the creation of humankind took place. This is noted in Genesis 1:26: "And God said, Let us make man in our image, after our likeness: and let them have dominion over the fish of the sea, and over the fowl of the air, and over the cattle, and over all the earth, and over every creeping thing that creepeth upon the earth."

It is fascinating to note the *us* in the verse above. It assures us that God is more than one being. It also shows the importance of humankind to God and how intimate we were with Him. He created thousands of creatures, yet He created humans in His own image out of dust and placed in us a living soul, as stated in Genesis 2:7. From the very beginning, God had an extraordinary purpose for humankind to fulfill.

It makes me question: What is that purpose, and how do we achieve it sincerely? And what level of spirituality did humanity posess with God in the garden? It is breathtaking to realize how close our makeup is to God's and how unselfish and loving God is to give us such a godly trait after He formed us from dust.

He went to the extent of separating the Garden of Eden from the rest of the earth for humanity's habitation. Then He placed everything we needed in the garden, and as the caretaker, He allowed Adam to name all the animals.

The Genesis story also tells us of the things in the garden that were created by God and given to Adam and Eve to have dominion over.

Genesis 1:28–30 gives us a description of the other creations—the fish, the birds, all living things that crawl, seed-bearing plants, and every tree that has seed-bearing fruits, all wild animals, and all the green plants that were meant for food.

Genesis 9:12 then informs us of how God feels about the other living things that He placed in the garden. It was after the flood in the time of Noah that recorded God's feelings: "And God said, This is the token of the covenant which I make between me and you and every living creature that is with you, for perpetual generation[.]"

Many times, as caretakers, we come across other creations and do not respect their existence. Some of us go out of our way to harm or even kill them without remembering how valuable they are to God and the purpose that they serve on the earth.

I

With interest, I note the snake that tempted Eve into disobeying God in Genesis 3:4–5 is a wild animal—one that Adam and Eve were given dominion over.

The question is, how did the snake gain so much godly insight to advise Adam and Eve, who had dominion over it? For that answer, let us backtrack and go to Revelation 12:9 to connect the snake to the devil. "And the great dragon was cast out, that old serpent, called the Devil, and Satan, which deceiveth the whole world: he was cast out into the earth, and his angels were cast out with him."

While God was setting up the garden, Satan was an observer. He had a claim on the earth because he was the first one here, and he envied the position that God gave Adam and Eve. The devil's sole mission from the beginning was to compete against God. Tricking or convincing God's creations into worshipping and following him was his purpose.

The newly created humans became just another prize for the devil to recruit and to strip from the bosom of God. He embodied the snake and spoke to Eve similar to how he would later enter Judas, who was at the Last Supper, after Jesus Christ gave him the morsel as recorded in John 13:27. "And after the sop Satan entered into him. Then said Jesus unto him, That thou doest, do quickly."

II

After Adam and Eve disobeyed God and He visited them in the garden, Genesis 3:8–10 informs us that, when they heard the voice of God in the garden, they were afraid and hid because they saw themselves as naked. Adam and Eve judged themselves for their disobedience by moving away from God. Humanity today indulges in the same actions when we knowingly go against the Word of God.

God placed a glory upon humanity during its creation. Our disobedience stained that glory, and we were not able to face the light of God anymore. It is this glory that Satan desires to rob from every person and to place him or her into a state of darkness. There is an inner desire in everyone to return to the originally intended relationship with God.

The snake received a curse due to its role in allowing the devil to use its body to deceive Eve into picking and eating the forbidden fruit. This curse could not fall upon the devil, who was responsible, because he was once one of God's high-ranking angels and was already blessed. God did not reverse his blessing, and instead, the curse fell upon the snake.

For reference, we can refer to Noah's son Ham, who saw his father's nakedness as recorded in Genesis 9:22. But because God blessed Noah and his family according to Genesis 9:1, the curse that fell upon Ham's son Canaan in Genesis 9:25 was intended for Ham instead.

Genesis 3:14–15 recorded the punishment that the Lord God assigned to the snake. In reading the scriptures mentioned above, we can distinguish that a part of it applied to the devil: "And the Lord God said unto the serpent, Because thou hast done this, thou art cursed above all cattle, and above every beast of the field; upon thy belly shalt thou go, and dust shalt thou eat all the days of thy life: And I will put enmity between thee and the woman, and between thy seed and her seed; it shall bruise thy head, and thou shalt bruise his heel."

After Adam and Eve committed their disobedient act and saw their own nakedness, as stated in Genesis 3:7, they sewed fig leaves together and made themselves aprons. In Genesis 3:21, God replaced those aprons with coats of skin before he banished them from the garden.

Genesis 3:22 helps us to better understand the primary reason why Adam and Eve were banished from the garden.

"And the Lord God said, Behold, the man is become as one of us, to know good and evil: and now, lest he put forth his hand, and take also of the tree of life, and eat, and live forever[.]"

Eating from the tree of life was the primary reason for their banishment. However, by following the scriptures into the New Testament, we will find that Jesus Christ came as the tree of life and brought us eternal life.

ꙨINTERVENTION

ꙨThe spirit of God remained with Adam and Eve after their banishment from the garden; this is evident because their two sons continued to make sacrifices to God. The firstborn was named Cain, and the second was named Abel. There is no reason for us to believe that the family of Adam did not know what type of offering that God required. However, it is noted that God found favor with Abel's offering but rejected his brother's. The question is, why was Cain's offering rejected? Did Cain give a better sacrifice to the devil instead of to God?

Cain became annoyed with his brother because God accepted Abel's offering and rejected his. Cain utilized the devil's tricks, lies, and murderous tendencies and lured his brother into the field and killed him. The evilness of Cain was passed on to his descendants throughout the Bible. John 17:12 described the son of perdition who has the tendencies of the devil's actions.

God's interaction with Cain was similar to how God called out to Adam and Eve after their disobedience in the garden. He asked Cain the whereabouts of his brother, and Cain replied that he was not his brother's keeper. As a result, God placed a curse upon Cain that he was unable to bear, and subsequently, he and his descendants lived an ungodly life. Some of them even boasted about their evil ways.

I

After the death of Abel, God needed to revive a godly lineage for the purpose for redeeming Adam and Eve's descendants who desired to serve Him. God blessed Adam and Eve with a third son, whom they named Seth, as described in Genesis 5:3.

Through Seth's descendants came a man named Noah, whose father prophesized in Genesis 5:28-29 that Noah would bring relief from their work and from the toil of their hands, concerning the curse placed upon the ground because of their forefathers' disobedience.

God considered Noah an upright and righteous man. He became tired of the wickedness upon the earth during that time and instructed Noah to build an ark. God told Noah that He would destroy all living things, including human beings and all creatures that were not in the ark. Then God flooded the earth for many days until all the humans and animals outside the ark had died.

The first covenant was between Adam and Eve in Genesis 2:16–17. The second covenant that the Lord formed was with Noah and his family, in Genesis 9:11. The lineage of the promised Son of God came through the descendants of Shem, who was Noah's son.

As we follow the holy lineage, let us refer to Genesis 11 and 12 to explain how God called Abram, who later became known as Abraham. This was when the whole earth spoke one language, and the people decided to build a city with a tower that may reach into heaven. The Lord came down and changed their speech to stop them from making the city. It was after this event that Abram's father,

Terah, started a journey to take his family to the land of Canaan, and when they reached Haran, they dwelt there.

In Genesis 12:1–2, the Lord called Abram and told him to leave home and to go to a place that He would show him. The Lord promised Abram, although he was childless at the time, that He would make him a great nation and bless him, that his name would be great, and that he would be a blessing.

Abram was an older man when God called him from his father's house and made him this promise. He accepted God's call and began his journey in faith. In Genesis 15:4, God told Abram that he would have a son, and to satisfy Abram's question, God told him to gather the following birds and animals as recorded in Genesis 15:9–10: a heifer, goat, ram, turtledove, and a pigeon.

In Genesis 15:12, God placed Abram in a deep sleep, and in Genesis 15:13, the Lord told Abram how his descendants would be in slavery in a strange land for four hundred years. Then, in Genesis 15:17–18, He created a covenant with him.

II

As Abram sat in his tent on the plains of Mamre in the heat of the day, he looked up and saw three men. Genesis 18:2–3 informs us of how Abram ran toward the men, bowed before them, and asked them if they wanted water to wash their feet and to rest themselves in the shade of the tree while he got them some bread. He supplied them with the water to wash their feet and the food that they ate, and the Lord was among these celestial beings.

In Genesis 18:10–11, the Lord promised Abram, although they were beyond childbearing age, that they would have a son. (It is through this son's descendants that the Son of God would come into the world.)

III

Let us now go to Genesis 32:24–28, and follow the Lord as He interacts with Jacob, who also was a part of the lineage.

> And Jacob was left alone; and there wrestled a man with him until the breaking of the day. And when he saw that he prevailed not against him, he touched the hollow of his thigh; and the hollow of Jacob's thigh was out of joint, as he wrestled with him. And he said, Let me go, for the day breaketh. And he said, I will not let thee go, except thou bless me. And he said unto him, What is thy name? And he said, Jacob. And he said, Thy name shall be called no more Jacob, but Israel: for as a prince hast thou power with God and with men, and hast prevailed.

My interpretation of these verses above is that Jacob did not wrestle with God in the manner of how two men would fight. He held on to God, pleading for a blessing, and he refused to let Him go before receiving it. He knew the value of a blessing since he and his mother stole the blessing that his father, Isaac, had meant for Esau, his brother.

The reference to Jacob holding on to the Lord and probably insisting that he blessed him is an indication of an acknowledged, sinful man asking for God's mercy.

In confirmation of Jacob's devious behavior, Esau describes him in Genesis 27:36 as a brother who manipulated him out of his blessing and birthright and caused him to plead with his father for another blessing.

Despite Jacob's waywardness, his descendent carried seed for the birth of the Son of God.

IV

After the Israelites spent four hundred years in slavery in Egypt, as mentioned by God to their forefather, Abraham, Moses was selected by God to lead the Israelites out of bondage. Again, to fulfill his promise, God Himself came down in His glory to talk with Moses and to instruct him about leading His people out of slavery as recorded in Exodus 3:1–6. I will quote verses five and six here: "And he said, Draw not nigh hither: put off thy shoes from off thy feet, for the place whereon thou standest is holy ground. Moreover he said, I am the God of thy father, the God of Abraham, the God of Isaac, and the God of Jacob, And Moses hid his face; for he was afraid to look upon God."

When it was time to bring the Israelites out of Egypt, God showed the Eygptians that He was more powerful than their gods, and He placed many plagues upon them to convince Pharaoh to let His people go. The final one was death to the firstborn children of both people and beasts. However, to protect His people from the final plague, God instructed Moses in Exodus 12:7 to tell His people to place the blood on the doorposts as a mark for Him to pass over.

As the Israelites left Egypt and entered into the wilderness, God's watchful eyes were always upon them. Exodus 13:21 recorded how God led them with a pillar of cloud by day and a pillar of fire by night.

V

God visited Adam and Eve in the garden, and the Bible did not mention that God's presence had any effect upon them. However, after their disobedience, they hid from the presence of the Lord. The glory that God placed upon them at their creation made it possible for them to stand in His presence. This is the glory that left them after their disobedience, and as a result, they could not stand in the presence of God. This was the glory that Jesus came to restore to humanity.

As the Israelites traveled through the wilderness, the Lord appeared in glory on occasion and effected Moses and the Israelites. On one event, as recorded in Exodus 19:10–12, before God appeared on Mount Sinai, He instructed Moses to sanctify the people on the first day and to let them wash their clothes the second day before He appeared on the third day. Moses was also instructed to tell the people that whoever touched the border of the mountain would die.

Exodus 33:11–23 records how the Lord formed a relationship with Moses and spoke with him as a friend. Moses felt that if he found grace with the Lord, and if the people were unique in the sight of the Lord, then he needed to see the face of the Lord. The Lord told him that no man could see His face and live. But to accommodate Moses, God placed him in a cleft of the rock and covered him with His hand while He passed by. Then God removed his hand and allowed Moses to see the back of Him.

Exodus 34:28–29 recorded that Moses was with the Lord for forty days, and he did not eat or drink. As he returned to the camp with the two tablets of the ten commandments, his face shone and Aaron and the children of Israel were afraid to go near him.

CPROMISE

AS WE CONTINUE THE JOURNEY OF THE SON OF GOD coming into the world, we will refer to some prophecies that were recorded to herald His coming so we can get a sense of His earthly descendants.

The Bible informs us that Jesus Christ came through the earthly lineage of King David. 2 Samuel 7:16–17 recorded the Davidic Covenant: "And thine house and thy kingdom shall be established forever before thee: thy throne shall be established for ever. According to all these words, and according to all this vision, so did Nathan speak unto David."

It is beyond human understanding to visualize an everlasting kingdom for Jesus Christ, who inherited the throne of His earthly forefather, King David, for eternity. And at the time that Jesus was on Earth, the Israelites were in exile. Therefore, the throne of King David was not active. This covenant informs us that God and humanity will sit on the throne forever.

Jeremiah 31:32–33 explains that the violation of the first covenant caused the need for a second. Hebrews 8:7–8 further expanded that, if the first covenant was faultless, there would be no need for a second—the one that was established by Jesus Christ.

I

Isaiah 7:14 prophesied the birth of Jesus Christ hundreds of years before He was born. "Therefore the Lord himself shall give you a sign; Behold, a virgin shall conceive, and bear a son, and shall call his name Immanuel."

Now, centuries after the book of Isaiah was written, Luke 1:30–32 records a conversation between the angel Gabriel and a virgin named Mary: "And the angel said unto her, Fear not, Mary: for thou hast found favor with God, And, behold, thou shalt conceive in thy womb, and bring forth a son, and shalt call his name Jesus. He shall be great, and shall be called the Son of the Highest: and the Lord God shall give unto him the throne of his father, David[.]"

Acts 2:34 recorded what David said about Jesus Christ, his descendant: "For David is not ascended into the heavens: but he saith himself, The Lord saith unto my Lord, Sit thou on my right hand[.]"

Matthew 1:19–20 records the circumstances surrounding Mary's pregnancy with Jesus Christ. She was betrothed to Joseph, and he was thinking about putting her away in private because he could not understand her pregnancy. Then an angel appeared to him to explain this extraordinary act and told him to take Mary as his wife.

This scripture is just remarkable and changed the course of humanity. A divine being, who is God and man, came through a woman's womb—someone who was created from dust—to restore us to His Father.

II

The devil has continued to hold humanity in sinful bondage from the beginning. He knew that God would send someone to free them. Like many people, he, too, was waiting and watching for a redeemer. Based upon the nature of the devil, he would rather murder the redeemer than have Him free the people under his spell, similar to how he manipulated the death of Abel in Genesis.

The Son of God's birth, at the time, was privy only to a select few. Zacharias was a priest, and his wife was barren. While serving in the temple, he saw an angel who spoke with him about having a son in his old age. This point is critical because his son became known as John the Baptist, the forerunner to Jesus Christ. At that time, the Jewish people did not have a prophet for centuries.

Although Mary was pregnant, she went to assist her cousin, Elizabeth, Zacharias's wife, with her pregnancy as recorded in Luke 1:40–42. "And entered into the house of Zacharias, and saluted Elisabeth. And it came to pass, that, when Elisabeth heard the salutation of Mary, the babe leaped in her womb: and Elisabeth was filled with the Holy Ghost: And she spake out with a loud voice, and said, Blessed art thou among women, and blessed is the fruit of thy womb."

III

Luke 2:7 records the birth of Jesus Christ, born in a humble surrounding that was shared by animals. Some shepherds in that region were notified of the Lord's birth by an angel, as stated in Luke 2:10–11: "And the angel said unto them, Fear not: for, behold, I bring you good tidings of great joy, which shall be to all people. For unto you is born this day in the city of David a Saviour, which is Christ the Lord."

The announcement to the shepherds was meant for many reasons. Some of them kept unblemished lambs for sacrifice in the temple. The notification of the birth of Jesus Christ to the shepherds may have also been meant to inform them that the baby, Jesus, would be the last sacrifice, and that there would not be need for other unblemished lambs.

Luke 2:13–14 records the extraordinary event that took place with the appearance of the heavenly hosts celebrating the significant effect that the birth of the Messiah would have on heaven and Earth. This event is also a confirmation that the spiritual and physical world share the same foe, who is Satan.

IV

Matthew 2:2 records how the magi, who recognize a star that represented the birth of a king and followed it, eventually visited Herod in search of the newborn king. As they left Herod, they assured him they would return to inform him of the whereabouts of the child; but instead, they returned home a different route as recorded in Matthew 2:16–18.

When Herod became aware that the magi had tricked him, he ordered the killing of all children two years and under from Bethlehem and the surrounding areas. His action fulfilled that which was spoken by Jeremy the prophet, as recorded in Matthew 2:17–18.

Herod portrayed the action of the devil as recorded in John 8:44, and his reaction is similar to the act that Cain performed with the killing of his brother Abel.

CREDEEMER

O T HE SON OF GOD BLENDED IN AND GREW IN WHAT was a typical family. Luke 2:19 records how his mother, Mary, kept His godly relationship a secret. "But Mary kept all these things, and pondered them in her heart."

The earthly parents of Jesus Christ participated in all the Jewish traditions, especially the ones related to Jesus. He was circumcised after eight days and presented at the temple as tradition required.

There was a righteous man named Simeon who waited around the temple to see Baby Jesus. The Holy Spirit told him that he would not see death until he had seen the Messiah. When the parents arrived with the child at the temple, the Holy Spirit directed him as recorded in Luke 2:27–31.

The prophetess Anna was also in the temple at the time that Jesus arrived. She never left the temple after her husband died. Luke 2:38 recorded how she gave thanks and spoke of Jesus as the redeemer.

Luke 2:44–52 recorded an event that took place with Jesus in Jerusalem when He was twelve years old. His parents were returning home from celebrating the annual

Jewish customs, and after a day's travel from Jerusalem, Jesus's parents realized that He was missing. They went back to Jerusalem to search for Him, and after three days, they found Him in the temple, sitting with the elders and learned men of the law, listening to them and asking questions. The men in the synagogue were amazed at His participation.

When His mother located Him in the temple, she asked Him why He did not return with them and told Him that they had been searching for Him. He responded with a question, asking her why they were looking for Him. Then He told them that He must be about His father's business. Afterward, He returned to Nazareth with them and continued to be obedient to them, but His mother kept this event in her heart.

I

The gospel of John records some salient points about Jesus Christ. John 1:1–3, record the following: "In the beginning was the Word, and the Word was with God, and the Word was God. The same was in the beginning with God. All things were made by him; and without him was not any thing made that was made."

John 1:10–11 further informs us that "He was in the world, and the world was made by him, and the world knew him not. He came unto his own, and his own received him not."

As we continue, let us reflect on another profound

statement recorded in John 1:14. "And the Word was made flesh, and dwelt among us, and we beheld his glory, the glory as of the only begotten of the Father, full of grace and truth."

I could not fathom the unconditional love that God has for humankind to go through such an extent to redeem humanity from sin and death by sending His only Son, a celestial being, to be born of a woman. Hebrews 2:9 records how Jesus lowered Himself beneath the angels for the sole purpose of suffering and death.

We are informed in Galatians 4:4–5 of the coming of Jesus: "But when the fullness of the time was come, God sent forth his Son, made of a woman, made under the law, To redeem them that were under the law, that we might receive the adoption of sons."

II

It is fascinating how the Son of God, who blended in with us, took on our sinful nature to redeem us. Matthew 3:1–12 records how John the Baptist was in the Jordan River, baptizing the people who came from Jerusalem, Judea, and the region around the Jordan, who acknowledged their sins.

Matthew 3:3 also mentions the prophecy of Isaiah, who spoke about John the Baptist hundreds of years before he performed a baptism in the Jordan River.

As John baptized others, Jesus came to him from

Galilee for baptism. It is important to note how John compared himself to Jesus as recorded in Matthew 3:11. "I indeed baptize you with water unto repentance: but he that cometh after me is mightier than I, whose shoes I am not worthy to bear: he shall baptize you with the Holy Ghost, and with fire[.]"

The baptism by the Holy Spirit, as noted by John, is a step to the missing link of the glory needed for the descendants of Adam and Eve to return to the presence of God.

When John saw Jesus coming to him for baptism, John's response was recorded in John 1:29. "The next day John seeth Jesus coming unto him, and saith, Behold the Lamb of God, which taketh away the sin of the world." Matthew 3:14–15, tells us that John tried to get out of baptizing Jesus, but Jesus insisted that it must be done to fulfill all righteousness. Again, it is important to note that Jesus did not commit any sins—and John knew it—but for Jesus to save us, He had to be baptized with water.

Luke 3:22 states that after Jesus was baptized and was praying, a voice came from heaven. "And the Holy Ghost descended in a bodily shape like a dove upon him, and a voice came from heaven, which said, Thou art my beloved Son; in thee I am well pleased."

Matthew 4:1 records Jesus's flight into the desert to be tempted. This is the most exciting event that causes one to reflect on the snake that was embodied by the devil that tempted Eve in the Garden of Eden. "Then was Jesus led up of the Spirit into the wilderness to be tempted of the devil."

This scripture tells us how vital the devil is on Earth, especially for those who do not know God. Jesus, who came to reconcile humanity to God, had to confront the devil because he is a self-proclaimed king of the earth. From the beginning, he tricked Adam and Eve into disobeying God and, as a result, held their descendants in bondage.

The devil was very confident of his position on the earth; however, he was not sure that Jesus was God in the flesh. This view is a reflection of Satan's pride and ego because he is continuously building up himself. Matthew 4:8–10 recorded one of the devil's requests: "Again, the devil taketh him up into an exceeding high mountain, and sheweth him all the kingdoms of the world, and the glory of them; And saith unto him, All these things will I give thee, if thou wilt fall down and worship me. Then saith Jesus unto him, Get thee hence, Satan: for it is written, Thou shalt worship the Lord thy God, and him only shalt thou serve."

The communication between Jesus and the devil is significant for us because it tells us that nothing is more important to the devil than being worshipped. He would do anything to achieve it.

ᴼPURPOSE

ᴼTO BETTER UNDERSTAND JESUS CHRIST, WE MUST trace Him as far back in ancient time as we can. I am assured and satisfied by John 1:1, where Jesus Christ, the Son of God, originated from. "In the beginning was the Word, and the Word was with God, and the Word was God."

He was in the Garden of Eden when all the drama took place. In the fullness of time, God allowed His Son to come into the world to redeem humankind of the sin that they inherited because of their forefathers' disobedience. From the beginning, the wisdom of God arranged the time, the place, and the tribe that His Son would enter into in the world.

Luke 24:44–47 records how Jesus spoke to His disciples of the prophecies about Him in ancient times and about His coming and His purpose.

John 8:56–58 also records a conversation that Jesus had with the Jews about Abraham's knowledge of His coming, which seemed so mysterious to them. "Your father Abraham rejoiced to see my day: and he saw it, and was glad. Then said the Jews unto him, Thou are not fifty years old, and hast thou seen Abraham? Jesus said unto them, Verily, verily, I say unto you, Before Abraham was, I am."

Genesis 14:18–20 recorded a meeting between Melchizedek and Abram, before he was named *Abraham*. Melchizedek, king of Salem, priest of the Most High God brought bread and wine for Abram. He had similar characteristics to Jesus Christ, as they both made offerings of bread and wine.

I

The Bible distinguished between the period of "the Law" and "the Grace" in John 1:17. "For the law was given by Moses, but grace and truth came by Jesus Christ."

Let us refer again to Matthew 17:3–4 to further explain the extraordinary meeting of men from different periods of the Bible. This meeting took place on Mount Tabor, which confirms the continuity of the Bible and how it extended throughout many periods.

In the meeting, Moses represented the Jewish Law; Elias represented the Jewish prophecy; and Jesus brought the good news to all the nations: "And, behold, there appeared unto them Moses and Elias talking with him. Then answered Peter, and said unto Jesus, Lord, it is good for us be here: if thou wilt, let us make here three tabernacles; one for thee, and one for Moses, and one for Elias." The Father allowed three of Jesus's disciples to witness this extraordinary meeting with Jesus and these two patriarchs to discuss with Jesus His mission that sprung out of their biblical journey.

To further elaborate on the continuity of the Bible, it is also fascinating to see how Revelation 21:12 mentioned the twelve tribes in the structure of the holy city of Jerusalem. "And had a wall great and high, and had twelve gates, and at the gates twelve angels, and names written thereon, which are the names of the twelve tribes of the children of Israel[.]" Verse fourteen mentions the apostles: "And the wall of the city had twelve foundations, and in them the names of the twelve apostles of the Lamb."

The final book of the Bible includes the twelve tribes

mentioned in the Old Testament and the apostles noted in the New Testament. How could people who compiled the books of the Bible, written over approximately sixteen hundred years, be aware of such detail? The Holy Spirit intervenes from the beginning to the final compilation of this historical book.

II

During the beginning of Jesus's ministry, according to Luke, He returned to Galilee in the power of the Spirit, and news spread throughout the whole region. Luke 4:16–19 records how He went home to Nazareth and entered the synagogue.

The ministry of Jesus highlights repentance and forgiveness for the sins that originated in the garden. It also strips the devil of his manipulative power that holds humankind in his sinful bondage and that produces diseases and sickness that is not in the Kingdom of God.

In Luke 9:1–2, Jesus gave His disciples the authority to cure these elements that are not a part of the kingdom. "Then he called his twelve disciples together, and gave them power and authority over all devils, and to cure diseases. And he sent them to preach the kingdom of God, and to heal the sick[.]"

In John 1:12–13, it also informs us of the status of the sons of God—which is given to those who received Him. I will highlight verse thirteen to stress an important point: "Which were born, not of blood, nor of the will of the flesh, nor of the will of man, but of God."

If Jesus Christ did not come, we could not be reborn as children of God. It is the point of being born again that Nicodemus questioned Jesus about in John 3:4–6 because he did not understand how a man could physically be reborn. It is also important to note that salvation must come through Jesus Christ.

III

As children of God, we are taught by Jesus in Matthew 6:9–13 about how to pray to the Father. "After this manner therefore pray ye: Our Father which art in heaven, Hallowed be thy name, Thy kingdom come. Thy will be done in earth, as it is in heaven. Give us this day our daily bread. And forgive us our debts, as we forgive our debtors. And lead us not into temptation, but deliver us from evil: For thine is the kingdom, and the power, and the glory, forever. Amen."

This prayer, which is given to us by the Son of God, Jesus Christ, included a prophecy about the earth and God's kingdom. The heavenly host acknowledges a part of the prayer mentioned here: "Our Father which art in heaven, Hallowed be thy name, Thy kingdom come. Thy will be done in earth, as it is in heaven."

The heavenly hosts are aware of the war that took place in heaven, and as a result, the devil and his angels were thrown out. The devil also continues to compete against the almighty God on the earth.

The angels are in waiting for Earth to become like heaven. In Luke 2:13–14, we get a glimpse off the excitement of the angels and the heavenly hosts as they appeared, celebrating the birth of the Messiah, praising God, and mentioning peace on earth. "And suddenly there was with the angel a multitude of the heavenly host praising God, and saying, Glory to God in the highest and on earth peace, good will toward men."

The Lord's Prayer also informs us that our Father resides in heaven, which is the highest place. Therefore, He is the true God because of the seat that He occupies, and we should worship Him because His name is holy.

The prayer also informs us that the devil's evilness does not exist anymore in heaven, and someday, the earth will be likewise. The prayer tells us that we need the Word of God daily, and because we are not perfect, we will ask God for the forgiveness of our sins while we forgive others of their sins against us because we are all imperfect people. In the prayer, we also asked God not to allow the devil to place insurmountable obstacles in our pathways, and we ask Him to protect us from his wrath.

The two greatest commandments mentioned by Jesus in response to the Pharisees' question, as recorded in Matthew 22:37–39, is also indirectly incorporated in the Lord's Prayer: "Jesus said unto him, Thou shalt love the Lord thy God with all thy heart, and with all thy soul, and with all thy mind. This is the first and great commandment. And the second is like unto it, Thou shalt love thy neighbor as thyself."

IV

God created us in His image, and He does not want us to indulge in the habits of the devil. From the very beginning, the devil was His adversary, and it always saddens Him when the devil manipulates us. Of course, He is a jealous God because He has an unconditional love for us. And like a good father, He never demands from us what He will not do Himself.

Genesis 22:2 illustrates instructions that God gave to Abraham to sacrifice his only son as an offering, and centuries later, God allowed this to happen to His only Son: "And he said, Take now thy son, thine only son Isaac, whom thou lovest, and get thee into the land of Moriah; and offer him there for a burnt offering upon one of the mountains which I will tell thee of."

After Abraham saw the place for the sacrifice, he left the donkey with his servant, placed the wood on his son's shoulders, and proceeded to walk up the mountain. Genesis 22:7–8 records the conversation between Abraham and his son as they walked up to the place that God had shown Abraham.

Genesis 22:13 informs us that God stopped Abraham from sacrificing his only son and supplied him with a ram instead. God tested Abraham's righteousness. Many centuries later, our loving God allowed His own innocent Son to carry a wooden cross and to be sacrificed on the hill of Calvary to save us from sin and death. There are many similarities between Christ's story and the events that happened with Isaac—who was also the only son of his father, Abraham, and an innocent child who carried wood for his own sacrifice.

V

The journey of disobedience started from the garden in the presence of God, man, and the devil, and it continued with the coming of Jesus Christ to remedy what took place in the garden.

The devil has continued to hold human beings in bondage and has been unwilling to release them, even at a cost. He did everything in his power to prevent the Son of God from becoming human and paying the maximum price, which was trading His life for humanity's freedom.

Freeing us from the devil's bondage required the Son of God, a divine person, who is both man and God. It is for this reason that God had to send His only Son. We know that the devil is an angelical being who is holding humanity hostage. The question is, how can a mere mortal negotiate this freedom from the devil?

Now we may better understand why Jesus Christ, who is more of an equal to the devil than we are, had to come to intervene on our behalf. This scenario is played out in Revelation 5:2–5. For brevity, we will write verse five: "And one of the elders saith unto me, Weep not: behold, the Lion of the tribe of Juda, the Root of David, hath prevailed to open the book, and to loose the seven seals thereof."

This scripture verifies that the arrangement of Jesus's death took place before Abraham attempted to sacrifice his son. The rivalry between God's people and the devil that eventually led to Jesus's death was indirectly hinted at in Genesis 3:15: "And I will put enmity between thee and the woman, and between thy seed and her seed; it shall bruise thy head, and thou shalt bruise his heel."

Jesus's entire earthly mission was to fulfill all the prophecies related to Him. Mark 11:1–6 recorded one of those prearranged events that is worth noting. He sent two of His disciples to go to a particular place where they would find a colt that had never been sat upon and asked them to bring it back to Him so that He could ride it into Jerusalem. Reading this scripture, one cannot help but realize that in verses five and six, whoever was responsible for the colt had some preknowledge to release it.

Zechariah 9:9 also recorded the riding of a donkey into Jerusalem many years prior: "Rejoice greatly, O daughter of Zion; shout, O daughter of Jerusalem: behold, thy King cometh unto thee: he is just, and having salvation; lowly, and riding upon an ass, and upon a colt the foal of an ass."

In Matthew 16:21, Jesus prophesied His death to His disciples. "From that time forth began Jesus to shew unto his disciples how that he must go unto Jerusalem, and suffer many things of the elders and chief priests and scribes, and be killed, and be raised again the third day."

⟨PASSOVER

THE PASSOVER INITIALLY TOOK PLACE IN EGYPT WHEN the Israelites were about to be freed from the Egyptians. It happened around the time when God was about to strike the Egyptians with the final plague: the deaths of the firstborn.

The Israelites followed the instructions given to Moses by putting lambs' blood on their doorposts, and they were saved from the destroying angel. They were also told to remember it throughout their generation.

In Matthew 26:18, again, I am amazed by the prearrangement for the Passover feast by Jesus. The disciples asked Jesus where He wanted to celebrate the Passover, and He sent them to a man. "And he said, Go into the city to such a man, and say unto him, The Master saith, My time is at hand; I will keep the Passover at thy house with my disciples."

At the Passover celebration, Jesus surprised His disciples by washing their feet as recorded in John 13:5. "After that he poureth water into a basin, and began to wash the disciples' feet, and to wipe them with the towel wherewith he was girded."

The reason for washing the disciples' feet must have been for some spiritual purpose, probably for the preparation of the Holy Spirit. Peter insisted that he would not allow Jesus to wash his feet, but after Jesus told him of its importance, Peter allowed it. The act of washing one's feet may have had the same effect as been born again, which was troubling to Nicodemus, who questioned Jesus. John 3:5 says, "Jesus answered, Verily, verily, I say unto thee, Except a man be born of water and of the Spirit, he cannot enter into the kingdom of God."

While Jesus was washing the disciples' feet, Judas, the betrayer, was also in the room. In John 13:18, He spoke to His disciples and said, "I speak not of you all: I know whom I have chosen: but that the scripture may be fulfilled, He that eateth bread with me hath lifted up his heel against me."

The last words in this scripture are similar to what is mentioned in Genesis 3:15: "And I will put enmity between thee and the woman, and between thy seed and her seed; it shall bruise thy head, and thou shalt bruise his heel."

It is just amazing how the first book in the Old Testament ties into the fourth book in the New Testament. The tying together of the Old and New Testaments is the continuity and authenticity of the Bible.

John 13:21–30 recorded how Jesus pointed out Judas as the betrayer. All the disciples were at a loss of who the betrayer may be. Then, Simon Peter nodded and made an inquiry about it to Jesus, and in verses twenty-six and twenty-seven, Judas is identified as the betrayer.

This feast of the Passover was very special to His disciples because they heard and saw things that had never before taken place at a Passover feast. The celebrant at the feast, who was Jesus Christ, gave them the bread as His body and the wine as His blood. To some of them, it may have appeared to be a paganist feast or even cannibalism. Luke 22:17–20 gives us further details of these events: "And he took the cup, and gave thanks, and said, Take this, and divide it among yourselves: For I say unto you, I will not drink of the fruit of the vine, until the kingdom of God shall come. And he took bread, and gave thanks, and brake it, and gave unto them saying, This is my body which is given for you: this do in remembrance of me. Likewise also the cup after supper, saying, This cup is the new testament in my blood, which is shed for you."

Moses received instructions from God while in Egypt to memorize the Passover. At the Last Supper, Jesus told His disciples to do the same. We are all invited to share in the feast of the Last Supper because it unites us with Jesus's body, suffering, death, and His resurrection.

I

John 17:16–19 records a part of Jesus's prayer as it relates to His relationship with His disciples: "They are not of the world, even as I am not of the world. Sanctify them through thy truth: thy word is truth. As thou hast sent me into the world, even so have I also sent them into the world. And for their sakes I sanctify myself, that they also might be sanctified through the truth."

Jesus's powerful prayer in John 17 was basically for His disciples and all of us who join into the faith. It amazes me how the eleven disciples (excluding Judas) faithfully dedicated their lives to preaching about Jesus and His resurrection after the Holy Spirit came upon them.

They never looked back at their old lives, including their families. Ten of His disciples died as martyrs, and one died a natural death. The washing of the feet most certainly contributed to their destinies.

After the Last Supper, Jesus went out to Mount Olive, and His disciples followed Him. Luke 22:40–46 described the grief that was upon Jesus in the garden of Gethsemane.

I can only imagine the weight of the sins that were upon Jesus in the garden. He was pure and not capable of sinning; therefore, the sins that He took on must have had a devastating effect on Him. Let us look at the impact that disobedience had on our forefathers in the garden and try to imagine how sin may have affect Jesus, who is God. Genesis 3:9–11 gave us some insight into the effect of sin on humanity.

The Lord God may have entered the garden as usual, called out to Adam and Eve, and received no immediate response. Then Adam explained that he heard the call of the Lord but hid because he was naked and afraid. Since Adam's appearance had not changed, the logical question was, how did he know that he was naked? His disobedience of eating the forbidden fruit affected the glory that God had placed upon him at creation. The guilt of his transgression diminished the glory placed upon humanity, and as a result, man can no longer stand directly in God's presence.

The weight of the cross that Jesus carried must have been light compared to our past, present, and future sins that He bore in the garden. Now we can better understand why He asked His Father to release Him from the suffering and death on the cross.

II

Jesus was arrested in the garden of Gethsemane by a mob, and they took Him to Pilate. John 1:11 reminds us of how Jesus Christ's own people disowned him. John 18:35 further confirmed how Pilate acknowledged how Jesus's people rejected him. "Pilate answered, Am I a Jew? Thine own nation and the chief priests have delivered thee unto me: what hast thou done?"

I cannot even begin to empathize with Jesus because it is all so depressing after first being betrayed by His disciple Judas and then by His people.

John 18:31–32 recorded Jesus's words about how the type of death He would endure was fulfillment under the Romans because under the Jewish Law, they could not execute Him.

It is our privilege to trace Jesus's earthly journey through prophecies or His words because we are in the position to compare them all. Mark 15:3–5 records how Jesus, in the presence of Pilate, did not defend Himself against the accusation from the chief priests.

Jesus's behavior in the presence of Pilate was prophesied in Isaiah 53:7: "He was oppressed, and he was afflicted, yet he opened not his mouth: he is brought as a lamb to the slaughter, and as a sheep before her shearers is dumb, so he openeth not his mouth."

Judas returned the money he received to betray Jesus to the chief priest and elders after the condemnation of Jesus, and then he went out and hung himself.

Matthew 26:24 records Jesus speaking about a warning to the person that would betray him. "The Son of man goeth as it is written of him: but woe unto that man by whom the Son of man is betrayed! it had been good for that man if he had not been born."

ᴏAɴᴄɪᴇɴᴛ Oғғᴇʀɪɴɢ

Tʜᴇ ᴄʀᴜᴄɪꜰɪxɪᴏɴ ᴏꜰ Jᴇꜱᴜꜱ Cʜʀɪꜱᴛ ᴡᴀꜱ ᴍᴏʀᴇ ᴛʜᴀɴ what the people present around His cross saw at the time. Some of the events that took place were similar to what happened in the ancient tabernacle hundreds of years before, as instructions given to Moses in the book of Leviticus.

These included some of the functions of the high priest and the offerings of the sacrifices that took place in the tabernacle. The scripture informs us that Jesus did not come to destroy the Law but to fulfill it. Therefore, I will attempt to relate some of the events that occurred to Jesus during His journey to the cross to the events around the ancient tabernacle.

It is significant to note that the veil that separated the Holy of Holies and the Ark of the Covenant is referred to in the Bible during Jesus's crucifixion. The high priest entered through the veil only one day of the year. The significance of this notation gives us a clue that the tabernacle was related to Jesus's crucifixion.

Let us look at some of the events that took place during Jesus's journey to the cross and His crucifixion. We agreed that Jesus died for our sins and to conquer death. His death was also intended to satisfy and to bring an end to the requirements related to the ancient tabernacle that was used before the New Covenant was activated. The torn veil in the temple after Jesus's death verified this fact.

The transition from the period of the Law to the period of Grace required the fulfillment of certain things. Matthew 5:17, for example, records what Jesus said about the fulfillment of the Law: "Think not that I am come to destroy the law, or the prophets: I am not come to destroy, but to fulfil." Some of the events that took place with Jesus's ordeal before Pilate, His crucifixion, and the offerings in the ancient tabernacle, noted in Leviticus chapters 6 and 16, are similar.

Jesus was aware of the actions that the soldiers were unknowingly committing around the cross and asked His Father to forgive them as recorded in Luke 23:34. He knew the people did not have a clue about what they were doing. "Then said Jesus, Father, forgive them; for they know not what they do."

Psalm 22:16–18 describes the events around the cross although they were written about hundreds of years before they occurred: "For dogs have compassed me: the assembly of the wicked have enclosed me: they pierced my hands and my feet. I may tell all my bones: they look and stare upon me. They part my garments among them, and cast lots upon my vesture."

John 19:32–34 supports this scripture by referring to the broken legs: "Then came the soldiers, and broke the legs of the first, and of the other which was crucified with him. But when they came to Jesus, and saw that he was dead already, they broke not his legs: But one of the soldiers with a spear pierced his side, and forthwith came there out blood and water."

Since Jesus was a sacrificial lamb, according to the law of the sacrifice, a broken leg would have disqualified Him as a lamb without blemish.

1 John 5:6–8 explained the significance of the blood and water that flowed from His side. "This is he that came by water and blood, even Jesus Christ; not by water only, but by water and blood. And it is the Spirit that beareth witness, because the Spirit is truth. For there are three that bear record in heaven, the Father, the Word, and the Holy Ghost: and these three are one."

I

Let us now return to the occasion when Jesus and Barabbas were in front of Pilate for Pilate to determine which one would be released. This platform was similar to what happened in Leviticus 16:8–10 by the high priest for the atonement: "And Aaron shall cast lots upon the two goats; one lot for the Lord, and the other lot for the scapegoat. And Aaron shall bring the goat upon which the Lord's lot fell, and offer him for a sin offering. But the goat, on which the lot fell to be the scapegoat, shall be presented alive before the Lord, to make atonement with him, and to let him go for a scapegoat into the wilderness."

Jesus represented the goat that was offered as the sin offering, and Barabbas represented the other goat that was set free for the atonement and send off into the wilderness. Pilate wanted to flog Jesus and let Him go because he found that He had committed no capital crime (Luke 23:22). However, the majority of the people insisted that Pilate crucify Jesus. Their persistence was similar to the casting of lots mentioned in Leviticus 16:7–8.

Jesus represented the sacrificial goat as he began His tortuous journey at the palace. Mark 15:17 records how the soldiers took off His clothes and clothed Him in a purple cloak. (Purple is the biblical color associated with royalty). Then they weaved a crown out of thorns and place it on His head, saluted Him, spat upon Him, and struck Him while pretending to pay homage to Him and called him King of the Jews. They then led Him to Calvary to be crucified.

II

Let us, for a moment, reflect on an unexpected, unimaginable event that took place as Jesus was sharing the Last Supper with His disciples, as recorded in Luke 22:17–20. At the supper, He took bread and gave it to His disciples and said that it was His body, which would be given for them. Afterward, He took a cup and said that it was the New Covenant in His blood that would be shed for them. I am sure that they did not think He would go out as a high priest who would sacrifice Himself for this covenant.

It is mind-blowing to imagine Jesus on the cross as a high priest, who is the principal celebrant in sacrificing Himself. Aaron was the high priest in the Old Testament who was installed by Moses, as recorded in Leviticus 8:5–30. The difference between Aaron and Jesus is that the Almighty God made His only Son the eternal high priest to be sacrificed on the cross, and at the same time, he fulfilled the offering requirement of the ancient tabernacle.

As I have mentioned previously, Jesus sacrificed Himself on the cross as an offering that took place in the ancient tabernacle. Leviticus 6:25–26 describe this offering: "Speak unto Aaron and to his sons, saying, This is the law of the sin offering: In the place where the burnt offering is killed shall the sin offering be killed before the Lord: it is most holy. The priest that offereth it for sin shall eat it: in the holy place shall it be eaten, in the court of the tabernacle of the congregation."

In verse twenty-six, it said that the priest who provided the offering shall eat it. We already established that Jesus offered Himself; hence, let us refer to verse twenty-nine, which informed us of who else should eat the sin offering. "All the males among the priest shall eat thereof: it is most holy."

Luke 22:19–20 recorded that Jesus told His disciples to eat the bread, which was His body, and to drink the wine, which was His blood, at the Last Supper before His crucifixion. The disciples were similar to the priestly line mentioned previously.

Leviticus 16:15 records how the high priest would make the sacrifice for the offering: "Then shall he kill the goat of the sin offering, that is for the people, and bring his blood within the veil, and do with that blood as he did with the blood of the bullock, and sprinkle it upon the mercy seat, and before the mercy seat[.]"

We established that the veil in the tabernacle and the events that happened on the cross are related. Therefore, while Jesus's body was physically on the cross, His Spirit was in the temple, performing the final rituals that lead to the torn veil in the temple.

Jesus, as the high priest on the cross, was stripped of His garment, and He did not have the privilege that Aaron had to take off his garments. Leviticus 16:23 informs us of further actions the high priest would take after the goat went into the wilderness: "And Aaron shall come into the tabernacle of the congregation, and shall put off the linen garments. which he put on when he went into the holy place, and shall leave them there." Let us relate Jesus's garment to that of the high priest's, who took off his own garment. John 19:23 says this of the soldiers' actions at the cross, "Then the soldiers, when they had crucified Jesus, took his garments, and made four parts, to every soldier a part; and also his coat: now the coat was without seam, woven from the top throughout."

Jesus was stripped of His garments at the cross, similar to Aaron's garments, which were left in the tent at the meeting mentioned in Leviticus 16:23–24. On the other hand, the burial clothes placed on Jesus were similar to the clothes that Aaron, the high priest, had put on after he had a bath.

Matthew 27:50-51 tells of Jesus's final moments on the cross and the torn veil in the temple. "Jesus, when he had cried again with a loud voice, yielded up the ghost. And, behold, the veil of the temple was rent in twain from the top to the bottom; and the earth did quake, and the rocks rent[.]"

Jesus, the eternal high priest, made the final offering for the cleansing of sins with His own body on the cross and in the ancient tabernacle. There was no more need for the once-a-year atonement as recorded in Leviticus 16:34. "And this shall be an everlasting statute unto you, to make an atonement for the children of Israel for all their sins once a year. And he did as the Lord commanded Moses."

Hebrew 7:27 also notes the significance of Jesus's death: "Who needeth not daily, as those high priest, to offer up sacrifice, first for his own sins, and then for the people's: for this he did once, when he offered up himself." The torn veil in the sanctuary signifies that there is no need for humanity to be separated from God any longer, and it represents the beginning of the New Covenant.

THE CROSS

THE CROSS THAT JESUS CHRIST CARRIED BECAME AN essential symbol to all of His followers. It reminds us of an innocent king who washed the feet of His sinful servants and who voluntarily gave His life to save them and to enable them to become more like Him. At the time of His crucifixion, most people did not have a clue that the purpose of the cross was to save them from their sins and death.

We are encouraged sometimes to bundle up our life's injustices and persecutions and place them on our imaginary cross that represents our king. The apostle Paul, in his writing in Galatians 3:13, said it best—although he did not physically witness Jesus's crucifixion, "Christ hath redeemed us from the curse of the law, being made a curse for us: for it is written, Cursed is every one that hangeth on a tree."

We could compare the cross that Jesus hung from as a symbol to cure sin and death to the pole mentioned in Numbers 21:8: "And the Lord said unto Moses, Make thee a fiery serpent, and set it upon a pole: and it shall come to pass, that every one that is bitten, when he looked upon it, shall live." Those who looked up at Jesus's cross and understood its purpose would begin the process of receiving forgiveness for their sins and the possibility of eternal life.

Some actions took place around the cross that went

unnoticed to the spectators because most of them looked through their physical eyes instead of their spiritual ones. The division of Jesus's garments into four strips by the Gentiles soldiers below the cross could symbolize that His gospel would go to the nations in four paths of the earth. Mark 16:15–16 tells us, "And he said unto them, Go ye into all the world, and preach the gospel to every creature. He that believeth and is baptized shall be saved: but he that believeth not shall be damned."

Jesus's seamless tunic, woven into one piece from the top down, which the soldier beneath the cross refused to tear, represented His New Covenant, and it is comparable to the ripped veil in the temple because of the establishment of this new agreement.

After Jesus implemented the New Covenant, God, Himself, tore the veil in the temple because it was no longer needed to separate us from Him. Mark 15:38 records the renting of the veil: "And the veil of the temple was rent in twain from the top to the bottom."

I

There were two criminals on their own respective crosses on either side of Jesus. One asked Jesus to save him and his fellow criminal, but the other accepted his fate and asked Jesus to remember him according to Luke 23:42–43. "And he said unto Jesus, Lord, remember me when thou comest into thy kingdom. And Jesus said unto him. Verily I say unto thee, Today shalt thou be with me in paradise."

There are many ways to interpret what Jesus said to this

criminal on the cross, but we believe that Jesus took him into an environment similar to the Garden of Eden. Despite such a horrific situation, the centurion acknowledged that Jesus is God and the people that came to see the spectacle smote their breasts as they left.

Also in the vicinity of the cross during Jesus's crucifixion, the gospel mentioned only His associates and a group of women, including His mother and one of His disciples. We are reminded in Matthew 26:31 of Jesus's statement to His disciples: "Then saith Jesus unto them, All ye shall be offended because of me this night: for it is written, I will smite the shepherd, and the sheep of the flock shall be scattered abroad."

II

Mary knew that her son, Jesus, was an extraordinary child who came into the world for a particular reason. She could not imagine the grief and the suffering He would endure, although she was told by Simeon in the temple as recorded in Luke 2:35, "(Yea, a sword shall pierce through thy own soul also,) that the thoughts of many hearts may be revealed."

Some of us could only imagine how the mother who gave birth to a divine person, man, and God may feel as she journeyed with Him while he carried His cross. Mary stood at the cross, helpless for her son, who was fathered by the Holy Spirit. I am sure that all kind of emotions went through her head. John 19:26–27 records what Jesus said to His mother and the disciple whom He loved at the cross. "When Jesus therefore saw his mother, and the disciple standing by, whom he loved, he saith unto his mother, Woman, behold thy son! Then saith he to the disciple, Behold thy mother! And from that hour that disciple took her unto his own home."

Let us reflect on how Jesus responded in Mark 3:33–34, before His crucifixion when His mother, brothers, and sisters were asking for Him. "And he answered them, saying, Who is my mother, or my brethren? And he looked round about on them which sat about him, and said, Behold my mother and my brethren!" At the cross, as Jesus looked down upon His mother, she was most certainly one of His disciples.

III

Now, let us reflect on the relationship that Jesus said He had with His Father as recorded in John 10:37–38. "If I do not the works of my Father, believe me not. But if I do, though ye believe not me, believe the works: that ye may know, and believe, that the Father is in me, and I in him." This scripture explains the intimacy between the Father and His Son and the relationship that is available to us through Christ.

It also amazes me how we recognize God but sometimes separate Him from His prophecies. These prophecies are God. Luke 21:33 explains the power of the Word of God. "Heaven and earth shall pass away: but my words shall not pass away."

Imagine Pilate after the chief priest insisted that he change what he wrote about Jesus. Pilate's reply is recorded in John 19:22: "Pilate answered, What I have written I have written." God's prophecies are by far more substantial than Pilate's spoken words. It is because of these written words that the Father took an observant position to His Son's sufferings. Although the burden was tremendous, Jesus had to endure the crucifixion process to resolve humanity's sin and death. It must have been a weak moment for Him when He cried out to His Father from the garden, according to Mark 14:36: "And he said, Abba, Father, all things are possible unto thee; take away this cup from me: nevertheless not what I will, but what thou wilt."

He again communicated with His Father as He hung on the cross, as noted in Mark 15:34. "And at the ninth hour Jesus cried with a loud voice, saying, Eloi, Eloi, la ma sabachthani? Which is, being interpreted, My God, my God, why hast thou forsaken me?"

Luke 23:46 says Jesus cried out with a loud voice to His father, "And when Jesus had cried with a loud voice, he said, Father, into thy hands I commend my spirit: and having said thus, he gave up the ghost."

IV

Many of us cannot even imagine the grief that the Father had for His Son's suffering because we believe that the Father is not capable of emotions. However, this entire event could not be real if the Father did not suffer from His Son's ordeal. God created humanity in His image; therefore, if we are capable of grieving, it must also be a trait of the Almighty God. The Bible records some of the human characteristics of the Father. For example, Genesis 8:21 informs us that God repented after destroying the earth with floodwater. Exodus 4:14 records that the Lord became angry when Moses found reasons not to be obedient. Genesis 30:22 also informs us of how God remembered Rachel and made her fruitful.

In Luke 3:22 and Matthew 17:5, we can see how the Almighty God verbally spoke from heaven and called His Son beloved. Luke 22:43 shares how an angel went to strengthen Jesus as He was going through His agony in the garden. These godly traits are also what human beings would experience; therefore, it supports the idea that the Father grieved for His Son.

CREATION

THE DRAMA OF DISOBEDIENCE THAT TOOK PLACE IN the garden is the primary reason for the entire Bible and the journey of Jesus Christ. Let us reflect on Genesis 3:17, which gave us an insight into how it started: "And unto Adam he said, Because thou hast hearkened unto the voice of thy wife, and hast eaten of the tree, of which I commanded thee, saying, Thou shalt not eat of it: cursed is the ground for thy sake; in sorrow shalt thou eat of it all the days of thy life[.]"

As a result of Adam and Eve's disobedience, God banished them from the garden. Hundred of years later, Lamech, a descendant of Seth, prophesized that his son, named Noah, would affect the curse that God placed upon the ground according to Genesis 5:29: "And he called his name Noah, saying, This same shall comfort us concerning our work and toil of our hands, because of the ground which the Lord hath cursed." I am sure that Lamech could not have imagined that his son Noah would build an ark, and that he and his family would be the only survivors after the flood.

Let us now discuss the curse that God placed upon humanity as recorded in Genesis 3:19. "In the sweat of thy face shalt thou eat bread, till thou return unto the ground; for out of it wast thou taken: for dust thou art, and unto dust shalt thou return." The curse of death came upon humanity because of the devil's influence of disobedience.

Hebrew 2:14 shows us how Jesus died to save us from death. John 11:25–26 highlighted the power that Jesus has over death in His dialogue with Martha, the sister of Lazarus. She was aware that her brother was dead and placed in a tomb while she spoke with Jesus, but she was unaware that Jesus was the resurrection and life.

In Acts 2:38–39, Peter spoke about what is necessary for us to return to God. "Then Peter said unto them, Repent, and be baptized every one of you in the name of Jesus Christ for the remission of sins, and ye shall receive the gift of the Holy Ghost. For the promise is unto you and to your children, and to all that are afar off, even as many as the Lord our God shall call."

I

According to the gospel of John, in chapter 20, after Jesus was crucified and buried, Mary Magdalene went to the tomb early in the morning on the first day of the week. She noticed the stone had been removed from the entrance. In a panic, she ran back to Peter and the other disciples and told them that someone had taken Jesus's body and that she did not know where they took Him.

When Peter and the other disciples returned to the tomb, they saw Jesus's burial clothes rolled up. Then the disciples left the tomb and went home. Based on John 20:9, they had forgotten about the resurrection. "For as yet they knew not the scripture, that he must rise again from the dead."

They were also reminded by Jesus in Matthew 12:40 about the resurrection when Jesus spoke with the scribes and Pharisees about a sign. "For as Jonas was three days and three nights in the whale's belly; so shalt the Son of man be three days and three nights in the heart of the earth."

Mary Magdalene remained in the garden, weeping for our Lord. As she looked into the tomb, she saw two angels, one at the head and one at the feet where the body of Jesus had been. They asked her why she was crying, and she told them they had taken her Lord, and she did not know where they had taken Him. As she looked around, Jesus was there, but Mary thought that He was the gardener until He spoke to her—and then she recognized Him. John 20:17 recorded the dialogue between her and Jesus. "Jesus saith unto her, Touch me not; for I am not yet ascended to my Father; but go to my brethren, and say unto them, I ascend unto my Father, and your Father; and to my God, and your God."

Based upon Jesus's dialogue with Mary, the disciples were, at this point, adopted into the family of God.

II

After Jesus's resurrection, He visited His disciples, but Thomas was not with them at the time. They told him that Jesus visited, but he did not believe them. John 20:25 shares the conditions laid out by Thomas for him to accept that Jesus was actually alive.

Jesus returned to them after eight days and entered through a shut door, and He stood before them and called Thomas to him. John 20:27 shows us the conversation between them: "Then saith he to Thomas, Reach hither thy finger, and behold my hands; and reach hither thy hand, and thrust it into my side: and be not faithless, but believing."

This scripture is very emotional, especially to people in our time who believe that God is asleep or dead. Like Thomas, even now, if we sincerely request confirmation that God is alive, I am confident that He will satisfy this request!

After Jesus's resurrection, He made several appearances. His encounter with Thomas recorded how Jesus came through a shut door. He ate with them, and it proved that He was not a ghost.

As we follow Jesus, we know that His Father is our Father, and there is nothing in the scriptures that tells us we will not eventually have some of His qualities—particularly the ones displayed when He entered the room through the shut door.

According to Matthew 28:19–20, when Jesus was about to ascend into heaven, He gave His disciples instructions and assured them that He would always be with them. With His ascension, Jesus became the firstborn to enter heaven as God and man. He was now ranked higher than all the angels and was given a throne next to His Father.

CONCLUSION

Even at the beginning of the world, the devil and his angels were among us. Most of us did not place great emphasis on them because, in many cases, we did not believe in their existence, or we were unable to see them through our physical eyes. As a result of this, they secretly manipulated us in their battle against God, similar to how the devil deceived Eve in the garden. The devil and his angels were known to God because they raged war in heaven and were eventually thrown out, as recorded in Revelation 12:9: "And the great dragon was cast out, that old serpent, called the Devil, and Satan, which deceiveth the whole world: he was cast out into the earth, and his angels were cast out with him."

To some, it may appears that the devil will have his way for eternity—but the devil is aware that there is a limit on his time, as written in Revelation 12:12: "Therefore rejoice, ye heavens, and ye that dwell in them. Woe to the inhabiters of the earth and of the sea! for the devil is come down unto you, having great wrath, because he knoweth that he hath but a short time." The devil is aware that God's love for humanity is unconditional, and he continuously rages his war of evil to destroy as many souls as possible. In some cases, he requests more power from God to inflict harm upon humanity to subdue people. A prime example is a dialogue that the devil had with God to prove that Job would be unfaithful if He took away His blessings from Job, as recorded in Job 1:11. "Hast not thou made an hedge about him, and about his house, and about all that he hath on every side? Thou hast blessed the work of his hands, and his substance is increased in the land, But put forth thine hand now, and touch all that he hath, and he will curse thee to thy face."

<h1 style="text-align:center">I</h1>

The Son of God completed His mission on Earth amid the devil and his angels. He is now seated at the right hand of His Father, in heaven. Luke 22:18 is a reminder of the words of Jesus, "For I say unto you, I will not drink of the fruit of the vine, until the kingdom of God shall come." Based on the writings in the book of Revelations, the kingdom of God will not come until the punishment of the devil and his followers is completed for the war that they started in heaven and continued on the earth. Revelation 19:20 shares the fate of the beast, the false prophets, and others: "And the beast was taken, and with him the false prophet that wrought miracles before him, with which he deceived them that had received the mark of the beast, and them that worshipped his image. These both were cast alive into a lake of fire burning with brimstone."

Revelation 20:10 informs us of the devil's punishment. "And the devil that deceived them was cast into the lake of fire and brimstone, where the beast and the false prophet are, and shall be tormented day and night for ever and ever." Revelation 20:11 talks about a judge sitting on a large white throne: "And I saw a great white throne, and him that sat on it, from whose face the earth and the heaven fled away: and there was found no place for them."

The cleansing of the earth became similar to that of heaven, noted in Revelation 21:1. It records the second coming of Jesus Christ: "And I saw a new heaven and a new earth: for the first heaven and the first earth were passed away; and there was no more sea."

II

The scripture notes Adam and Eve's banishment from the garden because of their disobedience. Now, their descendants—both living and dead—through the grace of God have an opportunity to return to the new earth. In the new earth, there will be no need for them to look out for the devil and his angels because they will not be a part of this new kingdom. The tree of life was protected from our forefathers in the garden after they committed the act of disobedience as recorded in Genesis 3:22, "And the Lord God said, Behold, the man is become as one of us, to know good and evil: and now, lest he put forth his hand, and take also of the tree of life and eat, and live for ever." Jesus Christ came to give us the eternal life recorded in John 6:54: "Whoso eateth my flesh, and drinketh my blood, hath eternal life; and I will raise him up at the last day."

About the Author

I am a retired accountant, a husband, and a father who resides in the Commonwealth of the Bahamas. My commitment to religious writing began almost fifteen years ago.

Although I am not a theologian, I feel that I have the necessary tools to spread the teachings of Jesus Christ to as many people as possible.

My desire is to one day reside on a farm on one of the beautiful islands of the Bahamas.

NOTES

NOTES

Printed in the United States
By Bookmasters